A Child's First Library of Learning

Wind and Weather

TIME-LIFE BOOKS • ALEXANDRIA, VIRGINIA

Contents

How Do Clouds Form?

ANSWER The sun warms the water in the ocean, in rivers and in the ground. As the water gets warmer, it turns into a gas called water vapor. We can't see it, but water vapor is rising into the sky all around us. After it rises, the water vapor cools. Then it turns into droplets of water and tiny bits of ice. When enough droplets and bits of ice come together, clouds are formed.

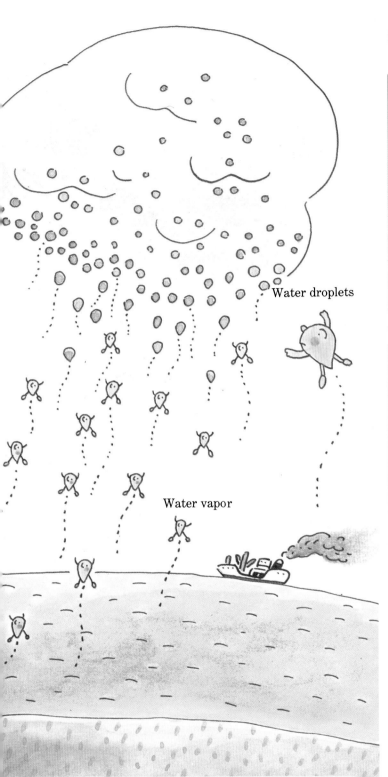

Water droplets

Water vapor

A Rain Cloud Forms

▲ A fleecy white cloud appears.

▲ More and more water vapor rises into the air, and the cloud grows larger and larger.

▲ Water droplets and ice in the cloud are forced upward. This produces a cumulonimbus cloud, or thunderhead.

❓ Why Do Clouds Have Different Shapes?

ANSWER Clouds form different shapes depending upon how high up they are. High in the sky they look like feathery white threads. Lower down they form fleecy clouds, like fluffy cotton. But height isn't the only thing that matters. The wind forms clouds into many different shapes too.

▲ Cirrocumulus clouds look like the scales of a fish.

▲ Cirrus clouds are feathery, as if they'd been swept.

Cap clouds often form around the tops of mountains.

Why Are Some Clouds Darker Than Others?

ANSWER Some clouds are thin and others are thick. Because sunlight easily passes through thin clouds, they appear bright or white. Light can't pass through thick clouds so easily. The parts where light passes through will appear white, but the thick parts where the light doesn't pass through will look gray or black.

The tops of the clouds are white!

Above the clouds

Below the clouds

Then Why Are Clouds Red in the Evening?

Sometimes at sunset dust in the air makes the sun appear red. So clouds look red too.

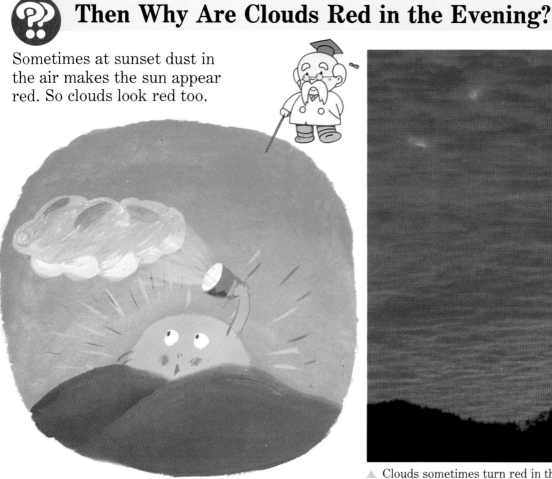

▲ Clouds sometimes turn red in the light of the sunset.

Clouds can turn other colors too

▲ These clouds shine like gold.

▲ These clouds look purple.

● **To the Parent**

Clouds have many colors depending on their thickness and the angle at which light strikes them. Rain clouds appear black because they are so thick that light does not pass through them. At dusk only the red light from the sun's spectrum reaches our eyes, making the sunset appear red.

? Why Does It Rain?

ANSWER Clouds are filled with water. Rain clouds have more water than they can hold. When a cloud has too much water it rains.

I wish it would rain.

Look! It's getting cloudy.

▲ These are rain clouds. It's going to rain soon.

▲ In jungles it rains a lot.

Above the clouds it's clear.

It's started to rain!

Our crops will live.

Whee!

Rain! Rain! Hurray!

Tell Me, What's It Like Inside a Rain Cloud?

Rain clouds are made up of many water droplets and small bits or particles of ice. When the particles get heavy enough they start to fall towards the earth. They gather water around them as they fall. The ice particles grow larger, and then they melt and fall to earth as rain.

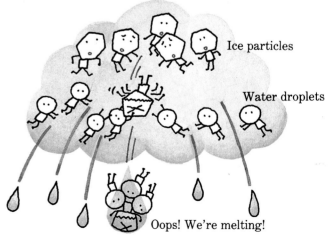

Ice particles

Water droplets

Oops! We're melting!

● **To the Parent**

Ordinary raindrops measure .04 inch (1.0 mm) in diameter. In a heavy rain, drops may measure as much as .20 to .25 inch (5 to 6 mm). An estimated one million water droplets in a cloud form just one raindrop. In light clouds the drops seldom become heavy enough to fall to the ground.

Where Does the Rain Go?

ANSWER Rainwater flows to lower ground, running along ditches and into sewers. Some of it sinks into the earth, where trees and plants will take it in. Some of it stays on the ground in puddles. But puddles disappear as the water sinks into the ground or rises into the air as water vapor.

A sewer pipe

● **To the Parent**

Some rainwater collects in puddles, some sinks into the earth, and some flows into streams and rivers, eventually reaching the sea. Water that goes underground may emerge later and flow into streams. Much of the rainwater left on the surface of the ground evaporates into the atmosphere.

12

Water that sinks into the earth flows downward along cracks in the ground.

TRY THIS

After the rain stops, make paths for the rainwater to flow in. The water will flow to lower ground.

Dig a hole in the wet ground and see how deep you have to go before a pool forms.

❓ Why Do Squalls Hit So Suddenly?

ANSWER Evening showers, or squalls, come from cumulonimbus clouds. That kind of cloud moves across the sky very quickly. One minute it may look clear, and the next moment the clouds have moved in. That's why evening showers come down on us so suddenly.

Hey! It's raining!

Hey!

Clouds That Bring Rain

◁ **Cumulonimbus clouds**
These clouds often move as fast as a car. They bring sudden showers.

◁ **Nimbostratus clouds**
As these clouds move in, the sky gets darker gradually, not all of a sudden.

◁ **Stratus clouds**
These low-flying clouds are very often the cause of showers. They sometimes touch the ground as fog.

● **To the Parent**

Light showers that strike suddenly on summer evenings are from cumulonimbus clouds. These summer showers, which are often accompanied by thunder and bolts of lightning, stop as quickly as they start. The clouds usually called rain clouds are nimbostratus clouds. They come in close to the ground and spread darkness as they cover the entire sky.

Why Does Lightning Flash?

ANSWER As thunderclouds get bigger, they build up powerful electric charges. When these charges become very large there is a flash. You see electricity jumping from one cloud to another, or to earth. These giant sparks are lightning.

We're little sparks of electricity.

Lightning is made of static electricity. Rub a comb with a piece of wool. Touch it to a piece of metal. Watch the sparks jump from the comb. Lightning works the same way.

▲ These cumulonimbus clouds cause lightning.

● **To the Parent**

Thunderheads develop from cumulonimbus clouds. Electricity is built up inside the thunderhead, then it is suddenly discharged into the air. Known as lightning, the discharged electricity has an enormous force of as much as several million volts.

❓ Why Does Thunder Rumble?

ANSWER As you know, the movement of electricity inside clouds causes lightning. That movement presses and bumps against the air around it, and that produces sound. The air that was disturbed first then bumps against the air next to it, and so on. That produces the rolling rumble of thunder.

When thunder is near, you can hear a sharp crack or booming sound. If it's far away, you hear a rumbling sound.

Why Don't the Thunder and Lightning Come Together?

If lightning is very close you hear the thunder at almost the same time. But if it's far away the sound of the thunder comes a few seconds later. That's because light travels much, much faster than sound.

Boom

Rumble, rumble

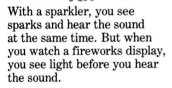

With a sparkler, you see sparks and hear the sound at the same time. But when you watch a fireworks display, you see light before you hear the sound.

Wow!

TRY THIS

You can use lightning and thunder to tell how far away a storm is. After you see a flash of lightning, check the second hand on your watch. See how long it takes until you hear thunder. Every five seconds equals one mile (1.6 km). Try again and listen as the storm gets closer.

● **To the Parent**

Lightning heats the air, causing it to expand rapidly and collide with the air around it. The sound of that collision is heard as a sharp crack if lightning is close by. If it is distant, the sound changes to a rumble by the time we hear it. In one second light could travel around the earth 7½ times, but sound travels only 1,088 feet (331 m). That is why we can see lightning before we can hear its sound.

❓ Where Does Lightning Strike?

ANSWER Lightning usually strikes tall objects like buildings and trees. Lightning will also strike metal objects, such as the metal tip of an umbrella. If you're playing in an open field or park where there are no tall objects, you should go inside if thunderclouds appear. If you're swimming get out of the water right away.

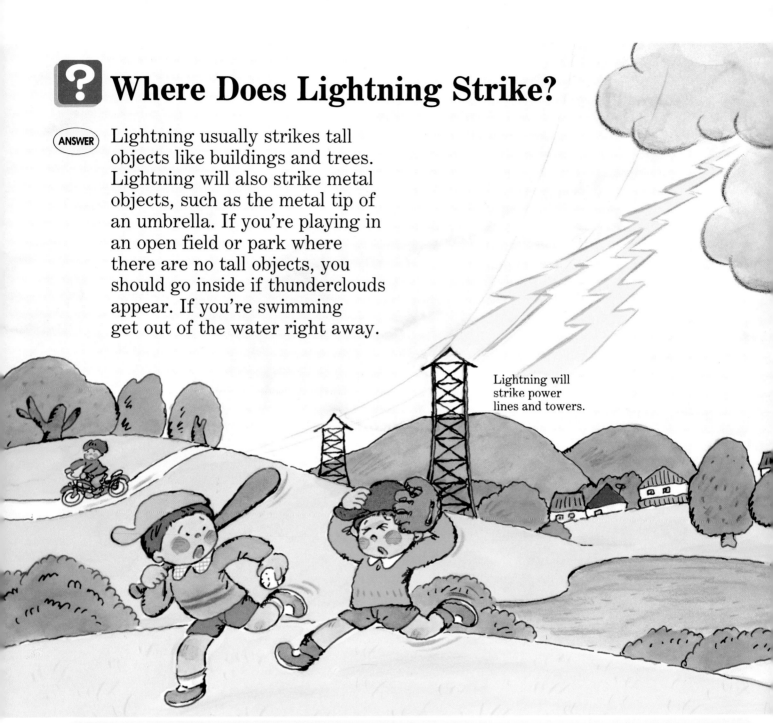

Lightning will strike power lines and towers.

Places where lightning is a danger

Avoid open fields, where you may be the tallest thing around.

Don't stand under a tree.

It may strike high up on a hill or mountain.

▲ **Lightning rods.** The rod on top of this country church passes the electricity in lightning into the ground without hurting anyone.

◄ A tree struck by lightning may be snapped off like this or burnt.

Places that are safe

Most large buildings are protected by lightning rods, so you're safe inside.

Lightning doesn't usually strike vehicles, like cars and buses, if the doors and windows are closed.

● **To the Parent**

When a thunderhead approaches, electricity is discharged by objects that are tall, made of metal or electrically charged. These are likely to be struck by lightning, which is an enormous discharge of electricity from a thunderhead. Such objects should be avoided when thunder is heard because the voltage in a bolt of lightning can easily cause death.

21

❓ Why Does It Snow?

ANSWER Clouds contain water vapor and tiny ice particles. When it's very cold the water vapor that is near the ice particles freezes. The particles get heavier and start falling. If the air on the way down is warm the ice particles melt and turn into rain. If the air is cold they stay frozen, and they fall to the ground as snow.

Ice particles

Snowflakes

If it's cold, the snow doesn't melt as it falls.

If it's warm, the snow melts and falls as rain.

22

❓ Why Does Snow Look White?

Light is reflected in all
directions when it hits snow.
That's why the snow looks white.

TRY THIS

The next time it snows,
collect a jar full and bring
it inside. Check the jar a
little later, after the snow
melts. See how little water it
takes to make all that snow!

● **To the Parent**

If the tiny particles of ice that
make up snow are very cold, the
surrounding water vapor freezes
directly to them without becoming
water. When these crystals fall
to earth without melting, then we
have snow. The sunlight contains
the seven colors of the rainbow.
Objects that absorb all colors
appear black. Those such as snow
crystals, which reflect all seven
colors, are seen by us as white.

Did You Know What Pretty Shapes The Snowflakes Have?

ANSWER Snowflakes, or particles of snow, have beautiful shapes and forms. The particles are called crystals. Ice crystals come in many shapes. When they form, the shape depends on how much moisture is in the air and on how cold the air is.

The photographs in the circles show crystals of snow. As you can see, their shapes are very different.

Snowflakes come in different sizes

When it's cold snowflakes usually are small. But when it's warmer snowflakes start to melt. They join other snowflakes and lose their fine shape. Many small ones stick together to form larger flakes.

That's why sleet has such large snowflakes in it.

When it's cold, snowflakes are small.

When it gets warm

they start to melt

and cling together

to make bigger flakes.

Let's look at crystals of snow

■ What you need

Put them outside
so they'll
be cold.

Magnifying glass

Black paper
or cloth

If snowflakes get
warm, they'll melt.
Wear gloves so
that won't happen.

Snowflakes will melt
if you breathe on
them, so cover your
mouth and nose with
a mask like this.

Catch the snow as it
falls onto the black
paper or cloth. Then
you can look at it with
the magnifying glass.

● To the Parent

The existence of snow crystals has been known for more than
400 years. There is a great variety in the structure of snow
crystals, depending upon the temperature and pressure of the
upper air where they form. Now that it is possible to create
snow crystals in the laboratory, the temperature and humidity
conditions in the upper atmosphere can be determined from the
study and analysis of the crystal structure of the falling snow.

Why Does It Snow More On One Side of Mountains?

ANSWER In winter cold winds blow from the sea to the land. They bring clouds that hit the mountainside and rise. The tops of mountains are cold and cool the clouds. When that happens snow falls on the side of the mountains facing the sea. Most of the snow is gone before the clouds reach the other side of the mountain.

In places that have a lot of snow, you sometimes can see snow piled all the way to the roof.

The clouds that brought snow to one side of the mountain disappear as they come down the other side.

● **To the Parent**

Cold winter winds blow across the northern oceans and pick up large amounts of water vapor. When they reach land the clouds come into contact with mountains, rise and become even colder. Most of the water vapor picked up over the ocean falls at this time as snow. When the winds come down on the opposite side of the mountain the moisture is depleted, so the snow stops, the clouds vanish and the weather is fine.

 How Do Icicles Form?

ANSWER When snow piles up on the roof of a house the snow at the bottom slowly melts and runs down the roof. As the water drips over the side it comes into the cold air and freezes again. This makes small icicles. As more water runs down the icicles it freezes on top of the old ice. In this way the icicles get longer and longer.

This icicle is so cold it hurts!

▲ **Icicles formed on the edge of a roof**

■ How icicles form

The heat inside the house passes through the roof and melts the piled-up snow.

As the snow melts, the water gets cold and freezes again.

Icicles grow longer as the water melts and freezes again and again.

▲ When a waterfall freezes, lots of icicles are formed.

▲ Water has dripped inside a tunnel and formed these icicles. They hang from the tunnel's ceiling.

● **To the Parent**

Because icicles are frozen run-off water, they form not only on the eaves of houses but also on stones near the outlets of springs, on the roofs of tunnels and around waterfalls. When snow is melted by the heat in a house or the warmth of the sun and the run-off water then refreezes, icicles form.

What Are Frost Pillars?

ANSWER When it gets very cold, the surface of the ground may freeze. The water under the surface is drawn up towards the ice. That pushes the ice upward. The water that was moving up then freezes. As this happens again and again, frost pillars, or columns, form.

CRUNCH!

CRUNCH!

▲ **Towers of strength.** Frost pillars have unbelievable power as they push upward.

■ How frost pillars form

Ice

Water droplets

The water on the surface freezes, and the water underneath is pulled up.

As the water under the ice moves up, it pushes up the ice.

The water that has moved up freezes, and more water is drawn upward.

Well, Then, Why Does Frost Form?

There's a lot of water vapor in the air. On cold winter mornings rocks and leaves are chilled. The water vapor freezes when it gets near those cold rocks and leaves. When it freezes it turns into a form of ice called frost.

▲ You can see beautiful patterns of ice in the frost that forms on window glass.

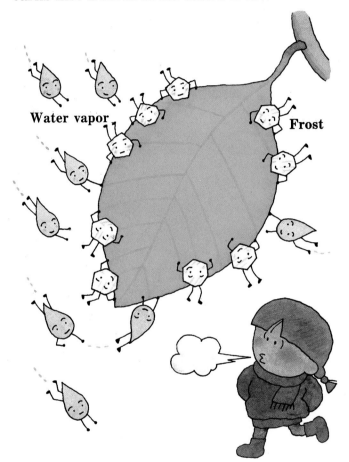

Water vapor   Frost

▲ **Frost on leaves**

 The pointed ends of the frost can be seen with a magnifying glass.

TRY THIS

Open the door of the refrigerator and look in the freezer. Part of it is white inside. In the air in the room there's water vapor. Whenever you open the refrigerator, some air gets in, and the water vapor in the air turns to ice.

● **To the Parent**

Pillars of ground frost form as water in the ground freezes. If the particles of soil are too small or large, as in clay or sand, the capillary action that brings water to the surface can not take place and frost pillars do not form. Automatic defrosters prevent water vapor in air from forming frost in refrigerators.

 When Does Ice Form?

ANSWER When the temperature drops below freezing, water turns to ice. You see lots of ice on chilly mornings. As the sun rises and the air gets warmer the ice turns back into water.

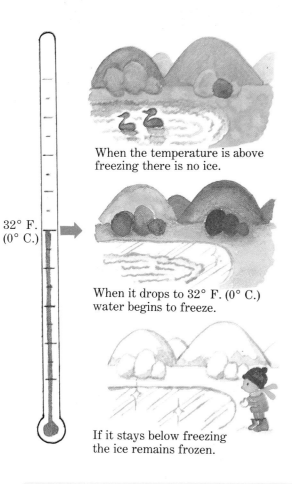

32° F.
(0° C.)

When the temperature is above freezing there is no ice.

When it drops to 32° F. (0° C.) water begins to freeze.

If it stays below freezing the ice remains frozen.

▲ This is from water that froze in a bucket.

▲ **A frozen lake.** In countries that have cold winters people can go
ice skating on the thick layer of ice that forms on lakes.

▲ **A frozen sea.** If it gets cold enough even seawater will freeze.
The wind blows the ice south, and it covers the sea's surface.

❓ What Makes Ice Melt?

ANSWER When ice is warmed it melts and turns into water again. Here you will see a few of the ways that ice can melt.

Having some fun with ice

Breathe through a straw onto a piece of ice. Because your breath is warm, it will gradually make a hole in the ice.

Ice cubes will stick together if you put salt on them.

If ice is in the direct sunlight it melts more quickly.

If a warm breeze blows on ice the ice will start to melt.

I see! If ice is in the shade it won't melt so quickly.

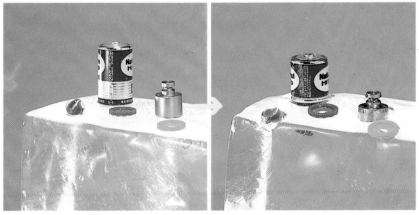

Put several different kinds of things on top of a block of ice. The heavier a thing is the more it pushes down on the ice and melts it. Gradually the object will sink into the ice as it melts.

● **To the Parent**

Ice will melt when the temperature rises higher than the freezing point. Before the invention of the refrigerator ice was highly valued. It was easily available in winter but was difficult to keep in hot weather. Ice was put into deep holes in the ground lined with straw, inside special icehouses or in other insulators.

❓ Why Can We Slide on Ice?

ANSWER When we walk on ice our shoes warm it and it melts a little bit. The water from the melted ice is what lets us slide. It's almost like what happens when you put wax or oil on a floor. Ice skates help us slide more easily on ice. Skis and sleds help us slide on snow too.

Ice skates are made in a special way so they'll slide better. You can slide in leather shoes too, or in any shoes that have a flat bottom. But the soles of boots are rough, so they won't slide very well.

Ice skates

Leather shoes

Gum-soled boots

• To the Parent

If you hold a piece of ice in your hand long enough, it will gradually slip away. The surface of the ice will melt from just the heat of your hand, and the film of water acts as a lubricant. Friction and pressure also melt ice when we walk on it, and that is why we slide even when it is below zero.

Why Does Fog Form?

ANSWER Fog is like a cloud that forms near the ground. It forms when warmer moist air passes over cool ground. When that happens the air cools, and water vapor turns to droplets. That's what makes the fog. We can often see fog in the morning because the ground has become cold during the night.

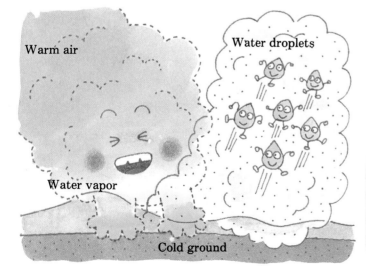

Warm air

Water droplets

Water vapor

Cold ground

● **To the Parent**

Clouds and fog are formed when the water vapor in the air condenses into water droplets. When this happens high up in the sky, clouds are formed. When it occurs at ground level, fog is created. Another difference is that water droplets in clouds are much larger than those in fog. Haze forms like fog, but it is not nearly as thick and allows greater visibility.

Fog forms in these and many other places

▲ Over cold ocean water it can even hide big steamships.

▲ It makes driving dangerous on highways in low places.

What Is Wind?

ANSWER Even though you can't see it, you know that air is all around you. When you pedal a bicycle very fast or wave a fan you feel the air in your face. Wind is air that is moving. We feel the wind blow when our weather is changing.

40

Why Does the Wind Blow?

When air is heated by the sun, it rises. Then cold air flows in to take the place of the air that rose. The sun heats the cold air and it rises too, and more cold air flows in behind it. This flow of air is what creates wind.

Cool air

Warm air

● **To the Parent**

Air expands when it is heated. The air that has expanded is lighter, and it rises. When this happens, the air pressure drops because there is less air. The cooler surrounding air rushes into the low pressure area. The rush of air is what wind is. Air contracts when it is cooled. Air that has risen is cooled. It contracts, becomes heavier, and descends to the earth, where it is heated to rise again. This flow of warm air upward and cool air downward is called convection.

 # Why Are Some Winds So Cold?

(ANSWER) In the winter, countries in the far north become very, very cold. Cold winds come from those northern lands and bring freezing temperatures with them. When these winds reach you it's a sure sign that the winter has arrived.

Cold north wind

Gosh, it's cold!

And How Long Does the Cold Last?

In the early spring warm winds from the south grow stronger. They drive away the cold, wintry winds. When they do that the coldest days of winter are over.

Cold north wind

It's warm!

Warm south winds

What Makes Hurricanes Form?

ANSWER Hurricanes form in warm ocean waters. As you know, warm water turns into water vapor quickly. Lots of water vapor rises from the warm seas. It enters the air, rises and forms cumulonimbus clouds. Strong winds blow the clouds into swirls. As the clouds get more and more water vapor from the sea they become larger. That's how a hurricane forms.

When more and more water vapor comes together, cumulonimbus clouds are created.

When water vapor cools, clouds form.

The water in the sea gets warm.

44

There is a strong swirl of wind
in the cumulonimbus cloud.

The swirl of wind
grows as it
takes on lots of
water vapor
from the sea.

What Is a Hurricane's Eye?

ANSWER When a hurricane forms, its clouds spin in a giant circle. In the center of the circle is a spot where there are very few clouds. The picture on this page shows you how a hurricane looks from above. You can see that the hole in the middle looks a little like an eye. So people call the center of this powerful storm its eye.

There are clouds all around the eye of the hurricane. The small dark place is the eye.

This photograph was taken by a weather satellite.

In the eye of a hurricane there are very few clouds and very little wind. No rain falls in the part called the eye.

TRY THIS

Stir the water in a basin around and around with your hand. See how a whirlpool forms in the water? In the center is an eye that is lower than the rest of the water.

Oh! There's an eye!

Look down on the water in the basin and you'll see an eye in the center. It will be the low part of the water.

● **To the Parent**

Hurricanes, created by strong updrafts of air, turn in a counterclockwise direction in the northern hemisphere. The center has no clouds. This center, produced by a strong downdraft, is called the eye, and it may be 20 to 30 miles (30–50 km) in diameter in a fully developed hurricane.

Why Do Hurricanes Bring Such Heavy Rains?

ANSWER   Inside a hurricane are a lot of rain clouds, and they bring the heavy rain.

▲ Sometimes sudden hard rains cause severe flooding. Going out in floodwaters can be very dangerous.

When a hurricane is near, the sky is covered with rain clouds.

Why Does the Wind Blow So Hard During a Hurricane?

Near the center of a hurricane the air is pushed up with great force. When that happens other air rushes in to take its place. That's why the wind is so strong.

▲ Strong winds make high ocean waves crash against the shore.

What Is a Monsoon?

ANSWER A monsoon is a strong wind that brings very heavy rain. During the monsoon season warm air currents flow from the tropical countries. The warm air tries to push out the cool air, and the cool air tries to stay where it is. The warm air pushes so hard that it rises high into the sky. There's a lot of water vapor in the warm air, so it forms more and more rain clouds. Finally the rain pours down from those clouds.

Cold winds

Ooh, it's so cold!

What takes place during the monsoon?

▲ Rice is planted. Because there's so much rain, the young rice plants grow very fast.

▲ When there's a lot of rain, rivers overflow their banks, and cliffs and hillsides come sliding down.

50

Above the clouds it's clear.

Warm winds

Ooh, it's so hot!

When warm winds blow we have summer

When the warm air finally drives out the cool air, the rain stops. Then there is summer with lots of dry, sunny days.

◀ When a lot of rain falls, the air is very humid. Mold forms easily, and food spoils quickly.

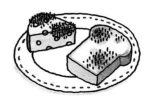

▲ Snails and tree frogs love rain. Many animals are very active during the monsoon season.

❓ Why Do Kites Fly?

ANSWER A kite rises into the air when the wind blows against it. But the wind has to keep blowing with the same strength. If it doesn't the kite will come circling back down to the ground.

❓ Then What's the Best Way to Fly a Kite?

Adjust the length of your string according to how hard the wind is blowing. And make the upper string a little shorter than the lower one.

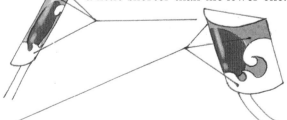

Run against the wind with the kite.

If the kite spins, put a tail on it.

● **To the Parent**

The wind does not rebound when it strikes a kite. Instead, the wind blows along with it. The strings of a traditional kite are attached so that the upper part is inclined forward slightly. The kite will be carried upward when the wind strikes it. The tail on the lower part of the kite acts as a weight for vertical stability so that the kite will not spin.

❓ Why Does the Weather Change?

ANSWER High up in the sky, the wind is always blowing, and clouds are always moving with that wind. As the clouds move across the sky, the weather changes. So it's really the wind that brings rainy or cloudy weather.

Let me help too.

Oh, it's getting cloudy.

55

❓ Did You Know That a Red Sunset Is a Sign of Fine Weather?

ANSWER The clouds that bring rain or hide the sun come from the direction where the sun sets. If there are no clouds in that direction the sunset will be bright red. So if you see a brilliant red sunset you know there will be fine weather the next day.

Here there are rain clouds in the direction where the sun sets, and the sun's rays are hidden.

Here there are no rain clouds in the direction where the sun sets, and the light is bright red and clear.

56

Why Do We Have Rain Even Though the Sun Is Shining?

ANSWER Sometimes it rains even when it's sunny and there aren't any clouds around. We call this a sun-shower. Strong winds bring the rain from clouds that are far away. Sometimes a sun-shower is rain that falls from very high clouds. The clouds disappear before the rain can reach the ground.

But Why Do Clouds Disappear?

Clouds don't often disappear just because they have turned into rain. When they disappear it's usually because the wind has carried them downward and they have turned into water vapor.

Look! The clouds have gone.

MINI-DATA

Clouds can float upward on winds that blow from low to high. When the wind stops, the clouds gradually come down again.

● **To the Parent**

Rain that falls when it is sunny and there are no clouds in sight is called a sun-shower. It may come from distant clouds and be carried on strong winds, or after the raindrops have formed the weather may change suddenly, causing the cloud to disappear. Clouds form where there is an updraft of air. When this updraft ceases, the cloud particles fall gradually. If a downdraft carries the particles to a lower level where it is warmer, the particles will change back into their invisible form of water vapor.

❓ Why Do Rainbows Form?

ANSWER You've noticed, of course, that you don't see rainbows at night. And you don't see them on cloudy days or when it's raining. Rainbows appear when it clears up after the rain or during a sun-shower. We see a rainbow when the sun's light is reflected from water droplets in the air.

On a fine day you can make your own rainbow.

▲ With the sun behind you, spray some water out of a spray bottle. You'll make a rainbow.

▲ When you make a soap bubble, you can see the colors of the rainbow in it.

● **To the Parent**

Sunlight appears to be white but actually is a mixture of colors. If sunlight passes through a prism it separates into seven colors. The prism refracts, or bends, light at an angle that varies with each color. Thus the red, refracted least, is at the top; and the violet, refracted most, is at the bottom. A rainbow appears when sunlight is refracted this way by millions of tiny drops of rain.

Why Are There Different Seasons?

ANSWER Some countries don't get the same amount of heat all the time from the sun. In the hot season they get lots of heat, but they get much less heat in the cold season. Let's take a look at the northern countries' seasons.

■ Spring

In the spring they get more heat from the sun than they do in the winter, but it's not as hot as the summer. The weather is just pleasantly warm.

▼ The leaves of an elm tree appear in the spring and have a pale green color.

■ Summer

They get a lot of heat from the sun. It's very hot then.

▼ In the summer the leaves of trees have a lovely deep green color.

■Autumn

They get less heat from the sun than in the summer but more than in the winter. So the weather is neither very hot nor very cold.

▽ In autumn most leaves turn red and yellow, and fall to the ground.

■ Winter

They receive only a little heat from the sun in the winter, so the weather is cold.

▼ The trees lose their leaves and sometimes are covered with ice.

65

? Why Are Breezes Cool in Hot Weather?

ANSWER A person's body is quite warm. It's warm enough to heat the air around it so that the air also becomes warm. When a breeze blows, it pushes away the warm air, and cool air takes its place. That's one reason why a breeze feels cool when it blows on your skin.

Warm air

Breeze

ANSWER 2 When we're hot we sweat. Sweat carries heat from the body into the air. It does this as it evaporates, or turns into vapor. That makes us feel cool. When a breeze blows, sweat evaporates more quickly. So that's another reason why we feel cool when a breeze blows.

Wind
There's no breeze in the house, and it's hot.
Heat

MINI-DATA

Laundry dries faster when the wind is blowing

When the wind blows, the water in the clothes turns into water vapor quickly. That's why the laundry dries faster on a windy day.

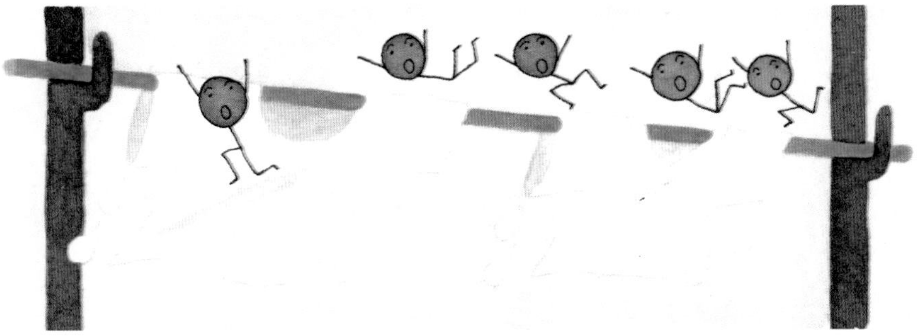

• To the Parent

The temperature of the body is almost always higher than the temperature of the air surrounding it. Perspiration cools the body by taking heat with it as it evaporates. This increases the moisture in the surrounding air, which reduces the rate of evaporation. But when the wind blows the humid air away perspiration begins evaporating more quickly again. For the same reason laundry dries faster when it is hung in the wind.

? How Does a Hose Help Keep Us Cool?

ANSWER If we sprinkle the ground with water, the heat from the ground warms the water. Because it's warm the water evaporates and rises. That makes the temperature of the ground and the air go down. And when the temperature is lowered, we naturally feel cooler.

The water that's sprinkled on the ground evaporates and takes heat with it as it turns into water vapor.

ANSWER

When water evaporates, it cools
the air. The cooled air becomes
heavy and moves around. The
moving air causes little breezes,
and those make us feel cooler.

● **To the Parent**

Our perception of heat and cold depends not only upon the
temperature of the air but upon the wind and humidity as
well. Even at an air temperature of 93° F. (34° C.), which
is close to body temperature, we will not feel so hot if
the humidity is low and perspiration can evaporate freely.
The evaporation of water sprinkled on the ground sets up
convection currents, and the air motion has a cooling effect.

 Do You Know Why It Hails?

(ANSWER) High up in the sky it's very cold, even in hot weather. In the upper part of the clouds the water droplets freeze into tiny bits of ice. Those bits of ice become hailstones. Because hail falls very fast it doesn't have time to melt before it reaches the ground, even in hot weather.

Small particles of ice melt as they fall. By the time they hit the ground they are rain.

Ice particles

But How Do the Hailstones Grow to Such Large Sizes?

As ice particles get heavier, they fall. But inside certain rain clouds there are very strong winds blowing upward. The winds are strong enough to drive the ice particles back up higher. More water droplets freeze and stick to the ice pushed up by the winds. That forms larger particles of ice. When this happens again and again, large hailstones form.

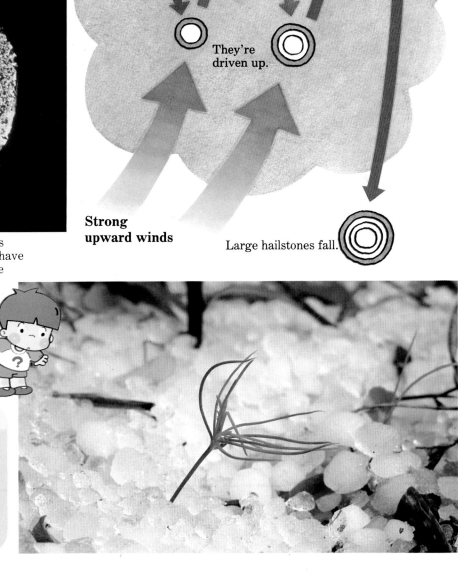

Droplets of water freeze onto the bits of ice.

They're driven up.

Strong upward winds

Large hailstones fall.

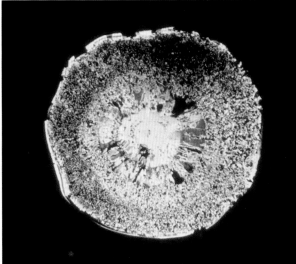

▲ If you cut a hailstone in half you see rings or layers, formed by water droplets that have frozen to it. We used a special microscope that enables us to see these colors.

▶ Some hailstones are so large they can break pine branches.

● **To the Parent**

Hail is ice pellets formed when strong updrafts in cumulonimbus clouds keep the pellet suspended in the cloud as it accumulates more and more layers of ice. When it becomes heavy enough it breaks away and falls to earth. Hail causes much injury to livestock and damage to crops, homes and planes.

 # Why Does Breath Turn White?

ANSWER The air we breathe out has a lot of water vapor in it. In cold places this hot, moist air cools in the cold and turns into small water droplets. The droplets look white, something like mist.

Water droplets

Cold air

Water vapor

Places where your breath will turn white when you breathe out

In a warm room your breath wouldn't look white.

In the sunshine your breath would not be white unless it's very cold.

On cold mornings in the shade it would be easy to see your breath.

 # Why Does Steam From a Boiling Kettle Look White Even in Summer?

When water boils, droplets of water are turned into water vapor. This is called steam. Steam comes rushing out of the kettle, but the air can't hold all of that water vapor. Some of the vapor forms small water droplets, and those are what look white. They are hot too!

● To the Parent

When the air can absorb no more moisture we say that it has reached the saturation point. The higher the temperature, the more moisture the air can hold. But even on the hottest day, if too much water evaporates into the air it simply cannot be absorbed. When this happens the vapor that is not absorbed remains in the form of droplets, which appear as white mist.

73

? What Makes a Shadow?

ANSWER When something gets in the way of a shining light, a shadow is formed.

If light comes from two places, two shadows will be formed.

If you run, your shadow runs too.

If you walk into a shadow, your shadow disappears.

I don't have a shadow!

Having fun with shadows

■ Don't step on my shadow

If someone steps on the shadow of your head, you lose.

Wait!

■ Shadow pictures

With a light in front of you, you can make shadow pictures. Make shapes with your hand, or stand with someone else.

Fox

Bird

Goat

Elephant

Dragonfly

● To the Parent

Light travels in a straight line. When it strikes an object it can not pass through, a shadow is produced. If the light source is weak, like sunlight on an overcast day, shadows are indistinct. In the shade there are no shadows. Shade is just the shadow of something already blocking out the light.

Why Do Shadows Get Longer or Shorter?

ANSWER As you move closer to the light, your shadow gets bigger. And as you move farther away from the light, your shadow gets smaller.

As you move away from the wall and closer to the light your shadow grows larger.

As you move closer to the wall and farther from the light your shadow gets smaller.

If you're right under a light, your shadow will be small. As you move away from under the light, your shadow grows larger and longer.

If the light is just above you your shadow is small.

But see the shadow grow if you start to walk away.

Some shadows are colored

If light shines on colored jars or glass containers filled with colored liquids, the shadows will be colored too.

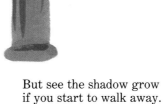

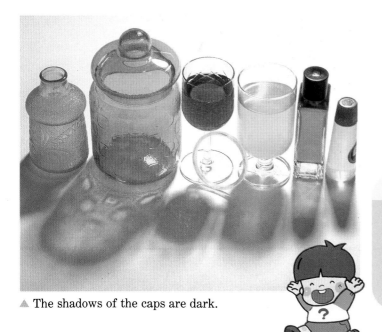

▲ The shadows of the caps are dark.

● **To the Parent**

Light from an electric lamp spreads outward. As a person or an object moves closer to the light source, and farther from the surface on which the shadow appears, the shadow becomes larger. If you stand directly under a light your shadow will be smaller because your body presents a smaller obstacle. As you move away a larger portion of your body blocks the light, and the shadow that it casts will become bigger and bigger.

Why Is a Mountaintop Colder Even Though It's Closer to the Sun?

ANSWER The sun warms the surface of the earth first, then it warms the air near the surface. The warm air expands, or gets larger. When that happens, it rises high into the sky, where it cools. That's why the land down low is warm but high up in the mountains it's cool or even cold.

Gosh, it's hot!

Why Is It Cool In the Shade?

The sun's rays are what make it warm outside. When something gets in the way of the sun's rays, we have shade. It's cooler in the shade because the sun's rays aren't shining there.

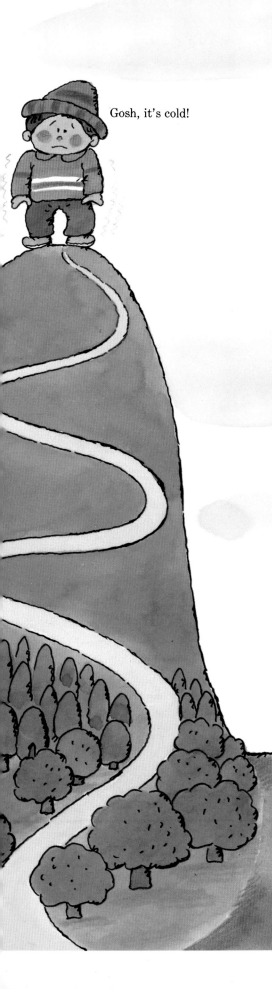

Gosh, it's cold!

A stone in a sunny place feels warm. But one that's been in the shade will feel cool.

● To the Parent

Objects or substances that absorb sunlight become warm. Sunlight does not have such a warming effect if it passes through something without being absorbed. Air is warmed only slightly by the sun. When it is warmed, however, it rises, expands in the upper atmosphere and cools down again. As air descends, it is compressed and warmed. Six to nine miles (10 to 15 km) from the earth's surface air temperature drops by about 1.1° F. (.6° C.) for each 100 yards (90 m) of altitude. Low temperatures in mountains are due to a combination of these factors.

 What Are These?

■ Frost forming a column on a plant

In the winter, ice forms on a dry plant. It looks like a frost column, or frost pillar.

In autumn it blooms.

■ Ice on a tree

When it's cold in the winter, trees turn cold too. If the water vapor in the air touches a very cold tree it freezes and looks like this.

■ The aurora borealis

This is the aurora borealis near the North Pole. When special particles from the sun strike the air, colors are produced. There's an aurora near the South Pole called the aurora australis.

Growing-Up Album

Record of Reactions to Nature

Children experience surprise and wonder as they
first encounter such natural phenomena as snow,
rainbows or lightning. Record these moments here,
along with your child's questions about nature.

● **Rainbow**   ● **Earthquake**

_____

_____

_____

_____

■ **Questions about Nature**

_____

_____

_____

_____

_____

_____

_____

● Snow

● Thunder and Lightning

● Ice

● Hurricanes

■ Questions about Nature

Mount a photograph here

What Are These Signs?

These symbols are used to show what the weather is like. Each symbol has a code mark under it. The picture with the same mark shows you what the symbol means.

♣ Thunderstorms

● Sunny

★ Rain mixed with snow

♠ Mist

Weather charts have special signs that indicate different kinds of weather. Some are shown here. From left they are sunny, partly cloudy, rain, cloudy, thunderstorms, mist, rain mixed with snow, and snow. For the correct signs where you live, have your child consult a local newspaper.

▲ Snow

■ Partly cloudy

◆ Cloudy

♥ Rain

A Child's First Library of Learning

Wind and Weather

TIME
LIFE ®

Time-Life Books Inc. is a wholly owned subsidiary of
Time Incorporated.
Time-Life Books, Alexandria, Virginia
Children's Publishing

Director:	Robert H. Smith
Associate Director:	R. S. Wotkyns III
Editorial Director:	Neil Kagan
Promotion Director:	Kathleen Tresnak
Editorial Consultants:	Jacqueline A. Ball
	Andrew Gutelle

Editorial Supervision by:
International Editorial Services Inc.
Tokyo, Japan

Editor:	C. E. Berry
Editorial Research:	Miki Ishii
Design:	Kim Bolitho
Writer:	Pauline Bush
Educational Consultants:	Janette Bryden
	Laurie Hanawa
Translation:	Ronald K. Jones

Library of Congress Cataloging in Publication Data
Wind and weather.
    p.   cm. — (A Child's first library of learning)
    Summary: Presents information about the weather in an
illustrated question and answer format.
    ISBN 0-8094-4829-7   ISBN 0-8094-4830-0 (lib. bdg.)
    1. Weather—Miscellanea—Juvenile literature.
2. Meteorology—Miscellanea—Juvenile literature. [1. Weather—
Miscellanea. 2. Meteorology—Miscellanea. 3. Questions and
answers.]   I. Time-Life Books.   II. Series.
QC981.3.W56 1989   551.5—dc19   88-37532 CIP AC
©1989 Time-Life Books Inc.
©1983 Gakken Co. Ltd.

Fourth printing 1992. Printed in U.S.A.
Published simultaneously in Canada.

TIME-LIFE is a trademark of Time Incorporated U.S.A.

Time-Life Books Inc. offers a wide range of fine publications,
including home video products. For subscription information, call
1-800-621-7026 or write TIME-LIFE BOOKS, P.O. Box C-32068,
Richmond, Virginia 23261-2068.